Bouba & Zaza

assess danger

ADEA
Association for the Development of Education in Africa

Michel LAFON EDUCATION

UNESCO
United Nations Educational, Scientific and Cultural Organization

Bouba came home from school. He greeted his grandfather and then his mother, who was cooking in the yard.
"You've put your shoes in your bag and you're walking barefoot again! Bouba, do you really want to get hurt? There are bits of glass and rusty nails on the ground. Next time…"
But Bouba had already gone into the house.

Suddenly his mother saw him standing on a chair.
“Bouba, be careful, you’ll fall! You should call someone to help you when something is too high for you to reach.”
“I know Mum, but Ibrahima didn’t want to help me.”
“Leave your big brother in peace. He’s doing his homework. You should have asked Grandpa.”

"Ouch, my finger!"
Bouba's little sister started to cry.
"Shh, shh, stop crying, before you get me in trouble and Mum yells at me. Anyway, it's your own fault because you always put your fingers in the door. Wait, I'll blow on it. There you are, all done!"
"No, it still hurts."
Bouba took his little sister in his arms.
"Come on, let's go and see Grandpa. He'll tell you a nice story."

Just then, Auntie and her little Fatou arrived.
"Look after your cousin for five minutes, I have to talk to your mother."
Bouba couldn't keep up with his sister and little cousin who had just found his bag of marbles.
"No no no, not in your mouth. If you swallow one you'll choke," said Bouba. "Careful Fatou, don't walk on the marbles, you'll…"

Then the two women heard
Fatou crying.
Bouba's aunt came over.

"What's going on, Bouba? You were meant to look after your cousin. Now run and get some disinfectant and a sticking plaster. Her knee is bleeding."
"But Auntie, I can't. All the medicines are locked in a cupboard. Mum says I'm not allowed to touch them."
Auntie got up and left the children in the yard.

Fatou was still crying. Bouba thought it would be a good idea to go and get her some cold water from the well.
“Wait, Fatou, I’ll get you some water.”
And that was when his mum said: “Bouba, don’t lean over. Get away from the well! You could fall in!”
“But…” began Bouba.
“Words do not come to us; it is we who go to fetch them” (we reap what we sow), said Grandpa.
Bouba did not always understand Grandpa’s proverbs but he knew that he’d better keep quiet.

"It's incredible. This child puts himself in danger every five minutes!" said Bouba's mother to her sister. "The other day he could have cut his finger off while he was making a slingshot with a long, sharp knife! And yesterday I found him at the top of a big ladder, ready to repair the roof as a surprise for his father."

"My dear, he's not the only one! Fatou almost gave bleach to her little brother to drink. She thought it was lemon juice."
"But did you leave your cleaning products in her reach?"
"No, I had just used it because I was doing the cleaning!"

At that point Zaza came into the yard. Her left hand was covered with a big bandage. Bouba went over to see her, holding the two little girls by the hand.

“Bouba, you’re looking after the children! You’re a really good boy! If only you knew…”

“What’s under that big bandage?”

“My hand got burned! I wanted to help my mum prepare a meal so I touched the cooker even though she had told me I was not allowed to go near it. It really hurts!”

“Girls, you see what can happen when you don’t listen to your elders!”

“I’ve learned my lesson,” said Zaza, looking at her hand.
“Little by little we become less small” (knowledge comes slowly but surely), said Grandpa, who was watching.
“And a ban! Can we touch a ban, Zaza?”
“A *pan*, it’s called a pan, little Fatou. A pan full of hot water or boiling oil is very dangerous! Mother must always make sure she turns the handle of the pan towards the back of the cooker.”

"And the squirt-squirt to wet the flies off my prate, Zaza?"
"*Get* the flies off my *plate*, little Fatou. No, you shouldn't use it, it can make you sick or it can get in your eyes – it stings you know! And if you use it near a flame the can may explode and set fire to the whole house!"

"So no ban, I mean pan, no squirt-squirt, and what about peanuts? What's wrong with them?"
"The chicken pecks according to the size of its beak" (choose what's appropriate for you), said Grandpa, laughing. "Because if you put one up your nose you will end up in hospital, Fatou! Ask your big cousin Ibrahima. He still remembers!"

Night fell. There was a power cut. Auntie and Fatou left. Zaza followed them.

“Mum, it’s dark. There’s no electricity. Where are the matches? I’ll light the storm lantern.”

“Matches? He wants matches now! You’re not allowed to go near the matches… Don’t think I am going to give them to you!”

Bouba’s mother lit the lamp.

“You must wait until you’re a bit bigger to do that!”

“Yes! The current is back on! Come on Mum, come and help me turn on the fan in the big room because I’m not allowed to!”

“Turning on the fan is not dangerous, Bouba, it’s the plug that you must not touch. You know, Bouba, I keep telling you about these things to protect you because I love you very much.”

"Me too, Mum, I love you but I don't keep nagging you!" said Bouba, laughing.
"To bring up a child takes a whole village," said Grandpa, taking Bouba in his arms. "My little lion, when you are big it will be your turn to warn children about dangers to avoid, and later your children will do it with their own children…"
"OK Grandpa, while we wait for that, can you tell me a story?"

Illustrations: Thomas Penin